KU-266-505

U2
RATTLE & HUM

U2
RATTLE & HUM

THE OFFICIAL BOOK OF THE U2 MOVIE

A
JOURNEY
INTO
THE
HEARTLAND
OF
TWO
AMERICAS

Written by

PETER WILLIAMS

&

STEVE TURNER

Edited and compiled by

PETER WILLIAMS

PYRAMID

Published in 1988
by Pyramid Books
an imprint of The Octopus Publishing Group,
Michelin House, 81 Fulham Road, London SW3 6RB

Copyright © 1988 Not Us Limited

ISBN 1 871307 41 4

ISLAND

The new album RATTLE and HUM
released October 1988
on Island Records tapes and CDs

The movie U2 RATTLE and HUM released
in the United States and Canada by Paramount
Pictures Corporation, and in the rest of the world
by United International Pictures.

Anton Corbijn: front & back covers

Back cover: Bullet the blue sky
Written by U2, Published by Blue Mountain
Music (UK) and Chappell Warner Music (ROW)

Photographers Credits
David Aron 46, 47; Tom Busier 40, 42 (left), 43, 44, 45, 81 (top left); Anton Corbijn 1, 3, 8, 9, 10, 11, 38, 48/49, 84, front & back covers; Colm Henry 16, 17, 18, 19, 20, 21, 23, 25, 27, 28, 29, 36 (lower), 33 (lower right), 54 (centre & right), 60, 61, 62, 62, 74 (top), 76, 77 (top), 78, 79, 80, 81 (lower), 82, 83; Keryn Kaplan 54 (left); London Features International 13, 14 (left), 22, 26, 30 (top), 31, 42 (right); Shane McCarthy (off screen photograph) 11 (top right), 14 (right), 30, 35 (b/w), 37, 39, 41, 93, 95; Jennifer Milne 58 (lower left); Paramount Pictures 32; Bill Rubenstein 6, 12, 33 (top & lower left), 34, 35, 36 (top two), 50, 51, 52, 53, 56, 57, 58 (top left), 64, 67, 68, 69, 70, 71, 72, 73, 74 (lower), 92, 74/75, 77 (lower), 88; Peter Williams 58 (top right & lower right).

All rights reserved. No part of this publication may be
reproduced, stored in a retrieval system, or transmitted in
any form or by any means, electronic, mechanical,
photocopying, recording or otherwise, without the
permission of The Octopus Publishing Group Limited.

Printed in Great Britain.

C O N T E N T S

When I get to the bottom
I go back to the top of the slide
Where I stop and I turn
And I go for a ride
Till I get to the bottom
And I see you again

Do you, don't you want me to love you?
I'm coming down fast, but I'm miles above you
Tell me, tell me, tell me, come on tell me the answer
Well, you may be a lover, but you ain't no dancer.

Helter skelter, helter skelter
Helter skelter

"HELTER SKELTER" by John Lennon and Paul McCartney
© 1968 NORTHERN SONGS LIMITED. All rights for the
U.S., Canada and Mexico controlled and administered by
SBK BLACKWOOD MUSIC INC
Under license from ATV MUSIC (MACLEN). All rights reserved.
International copyright secured. Used by permission.

> "America both fascinates me and frightens me, I can't get it out of my system."
>
> Bono.

April, 1987 in the U.S.A. and U2 are on the covers of *Time, Musician,* and *Rolling Stone. The Joshua Tree* has become America's best selling album. *With or Without You* is the best selling single. Night after night U2 are playing live to capacity houses, embracing the American audiences, as the American audiences embrace them.

This is a band approaching the heights of acclaim. Everything they've worked for during the long tours of the early Eighties is finally happening. Before they ever touched the shores of America Bono was cheekily bracket-

ing U2 with Elvis, The Beatles and The Stones. Now it's everyone else that's doing the New Beatles talk.

Television commentators chatter breezily about a a return of Sixties social concern. A New York ticket vendor compares the appetite of his customers with that of "Beatlemaniacs". The accolade of *Time's* front cover puts them up there with The Beatles, The Band and The Who.

The Joshua Tree album seems set in an essentially American landscape. Back home in Europe, press and public alike are unsure

Why America?

about the connections. Rumours filter back that U2 have been playing Country and Western music, Blues music. Even the photographs and images seem to be American, and so much of the tour is in the U.S.A. Questions arise; Why America? Why the new music?

"America both fascinates me and frightens me," says Bono, "I can't get it out of my system. The German film maker Wim Wenders, who directed *Paris, Texas*, has said that America has colonised our unconscious. He's right. America is everywhere. You don't even have to go there — it comes to you. No

matter where we live it's pumped into our homes in *Dallas, Dynasty* and *Hill Street Blues*. It's Hollywood, it's Coca-Cola, it's Levi's, it's Harley Davidsons. There's good and bad in all of these, but either way you've got to deal with it.

"Growing up in Ireland, I was aware of America as a super-real place. It was as though it might not really exist. It might only exist on the television and when I turned off the television America would just disappear. When I got to America I found it was just as super-real as it was on T.V. I remember that

television was true to life. People were shooting each other dead on the streets and all that. In L.A. there's a gangland murder every day. There was the dream and the nightmare, side by side."

U2 have talked about two Americas, and now amid the chaos of the tour they are exploring both. Their daily routine on the road is filled with the apparent glamour of the celebrity lifestyle, but they endeavour to keep in touch with life on the other side of the tracks.

For Bono as a writer, venturing out under

cover is necessary for him now because the America he sees in the course of his work is not the America that fires his imagination. Work means the interiors of aeroplanes, secluded hotel suites, press conferences, soundchecks. Yet his inspiration has always come from the street, from the people who face the storms of life without protection.

U2's hope is to discover the mythical America that they fell in love with from rhythm & blues songs, Flannery O'Connor's fiction and James Agee's documentary classic of Southern tenant farmers *Let Us Now Praise*

Famous Men.

The band have been meeting graffiti artists in San Francisco, refugees from Central America, and writing songs set in a Skid Row hotel in Los Angeles where they shot a video earlier in the year. In his bags, Bono carries the results of the tour's plundering of book stores and record stores. He talks about the short stories of Raymond Carver and the poetry of Charles Bukowski, men who have in different ways explored the underbelly of America, the lives of quiet desperation, the bad skin beneath the make up.

San Francisco.

> "To me Elvis is the symbol of everything good and bad about America."
>
> Bono.

The ghost of Elvis haunts Memphis and has started to haunt Bono. Back in the early 1950s as a precocious teenager newly moved from rural Mississippi, Elvis had begun his own voyage of discovery, tuning in to the local country radio, checking out blues on Beale Street, attending white gospel sing-ins at the Ellis Auditorium and visiting the *Old Time Camp Meeting Of The Air* at East Trigg Baptist Church, where he heard the likes of Mahalia Jackson and Marion Williams.

His genius was to make a new music out of the music he loved. In adopting the style and the movements of a streetwise black gangster and the music of the poor rural negro Elvis had started a process of cultural desegregation. Through rock & roll, young whites came to know and respect black American culture and, through that, black African culture. It still needed a Martin Luther King to push for changes on the statute books but the movement that Elvis began certainly loosened the cement in the wall between black and white.

"To me Elvis is the symbol of everything

Elvis Presley and the two Americas

good and bad about America," Bono comments. "Here was this guy from Memphis and he's just a poor boy living in a shack, whose twin brother died at birth. He grows up and becomes the most popular performer in America. He has untold riches and becomes The King.

"Isn't that what America is all about? You can be a peasant and end up in the palace. Yet it's the very thing that killed him. He got everything he wanted but it wasn't what he needed."

On U2's album *The Unforgettable Fire* two American heroes were celebrated — Elvis Presley and Martin Luther King. Both men were inspirations to a generation. Both died in Memphis — but what different deaths.

King was gunned down on the balcony of his motel, a victim of those who didn't want to see justice progressing so fast. A victim of the hatred directed towards someone whose life burned with a passion to see the blessings of life more evenly distributed.

Elvis died in his bathroom, a victim of self-gratification. A victim of ice cream, drugs, television, Hollywood, supermarket religion and all the other things we're told we have the right as free people to please ourselves with.

Maybe these are the two Americas U2 are trying to identify.

Larry at the Graceland Grave.

Angel of Harlem

It was a cold and wet December day
When we touched the ground at JFK
The snow was melting on the ground
On BLS we heard the sound
Of an angel

New York like a Christmas tree
I said tonight this city belongs to me
And an angel

Soul love, this love won't let me go
So long, angel of Harlem

Birdland on 53
The street sounds like a symphony
We got John Coltrane and A Love Supreme
Miles and she's got to be
An angel

Lady Day got diamond eyes
She sees the truth behind the lies
Angel

Soul love, this love won't let me go
So long, angel of Harlem

Blue light on the avenue
God knows they got to you
An empty glass, the lady sings
Eyes swollen like a bee sting
Blinded you lost your way
On the side streets and the alleyways
Like a star exploding in the night
Falling to the city and the silver light
An angel in devils shoes
Salvation in the Blues
Though you never looked like an angel
Angel of Harlem

Written by U2, Published by Blue Mountain Music (UK) and
Chappell Warner Music (ROW).

> *"People get into bands for all the wrong reasons."*
>
> Bono.

Dublin, Ireland is home for U2. It always has been and, despite their success, it always will be. Living and working in Dublin has kept U2 away from the rat-race of the music business. Particularly in earlier years, this was a vital part of forming U2's self-sufficient attitude towards the rest of the record industry. Moving into the 1990s, Dublin now possesses one of the world's most prolific music scenes, of which U2 are proud to be a part.

If success has given U2 anything, it is freedom to experiment. The band are briefly in Dublin to film some sequences for *Rattle & Hum.* The idea is to record some new songs, but instead of using Windmill Lane studios, the recording is to be done in a deserted railway depot on the opposite bank of the River Liffey.

All of the equipment is arranged up on a large balcony area within the depot, avoiding the places where the rain comes through the roof. A mobile recording studio has been brought in, with Jimmy Iovine as producer. Jimmy seems pleased with the very "live" sound of the warehouse space, particularly the

Dublin

drum sound. This isn't a video set up with miming to play-back; this is for real, playing and recording live.

U2 are here to record two songs against the backdrop of dusty white walls and grey steel girders. The first is *Desire* a song about ambition, maybe even the ambition to be in a band.

"People get into bands for all the wrong reasons," says Bono. "You don't join a band to save the world but to save your own ass and get off the streets. You want to get out of the crowd — to play to the crowd rather than to be in the crowd. All the wrong reasons.

"So this is a song about ambition. I wanted to own up to that because people look at U2 and they see all these pure motives, yet we started off being in a band for the most impure motives of anyone. We started off through just being bored at school, through not wanting to get a job in a factory or to be a schoolteacher or join the army or whatever. That's not where we've ended up, but it's where we started."

Desire is strung around a Bo Diddley beat, the sort of pounding that Buddy Holly incorporated into *Not Fade Away*. "We talked about getting some songs with interesting drum lines," says Larry, "so instead of spending time jamming as we used to, we each went away and did research and came back. This is what we came up with."

Bono sees *Desire* as a step towards a rock & roll single. "I think that because people now play us on the radio we have a duty to make sure that what they play is a little bit at odds with everything else," he says. "We want to use our position — or in this case abuse our position. We can make a rock & roll 45 that they wouldn't play on the radio if it was by an unknown group. We can get it on the radio, so let's get it on the radio!"

"Those early American rock & rollers like Buddy Holly, Eddie Cochran and Gene Vincent — their songs were so complete. They used one single idea, put it to a backbeat and repeated it. The hypnosis of that was incredible and we found that we could write that kind of stuff quite easily. *Desire* is one of those songs."

"Red Guitar, on Fire – Desire."

Written by U2, Published by Blue Mountain Music (UK) and Chappell Warner Music (ROW).

22

Elvis

Hendrix

Dylan

Richards

> *"There's no way that we're turning into a revivalist band"*
>
> The Edge

Six albums into their career, U2 are at the point where the Beatles moved from *Revolver* to *Sgt. Pepper*, Bob Dylan from *Highway 61 Revisited* to *Blonde on Blonde*, Bruce Springsteen from *Nebraska* to *Born in The USA*. It's a time of transition. A time to assess where you've come from and where you intend to go. At this point U2 are neither jaded nor faded, attacking everything with the enthusiasm that must have been there the day they first got together.

As Adam says, "We knew before we took on the *Joshua Tree* tour that it was going to be tough and we'd have to keep our heads together if we weren't going to let it overwhelm us. *The Joshua Tree* gave us a position to get to a larger audience and musically we now have the freedom to do whatever we like."

Since the tour started, U2 have been diving into America's musical heritage, listening to gospel and blues, country and cajun, becoming entranced with men like Elvis Presley for the first time, writing songs with men like Roy Orbison and B.B. King in mind.

Discovering New Music

"We're sold this idea that the music we should be listening to should always be today's music," Bono continues. "Why? Why listen to nowadays? To stay in touch? But to stay in touch with what? Records haven't got any better. As soon as I'd run out of records to play that were of the present I started looking into the past."

U2 had served no apprenticeship. Their influences had been the music they grew up with — David Bowie, Roxy Music, The Stones and later Patti Smith, Tom Verlaine and Television. They'd started composing their own songs because they found cover versions beyond their fledgling skills. The Edge recalls, "In the early years when it came to writing our own songs our attitude was, if Television and Patti Smith can be original, why can't we?"

Says Bono, "We created U2 out of ourselves. Out of the four of us. We weren't listening to Irish music, let alone American music. There was a feeling of having a record collection that started in 1976 and a rough idea of what blues and country was. That's where we came out of. . .nowhere."

This didn't seem to matter for a while. Their sound was triumphant and original. It couldn't easily be described in terms of the immediate past or the long distant past. "Up to that point that felt exciting,"admits Bono. "That was what was exciting about U2, but it was also incredibly isolating. We didn't feel a

The King "Elvis Presley" and The King "B. B. King" on Beale Street, Memphis, Tennessee 1956.

part of anything, musically speaking."

He felt this isolation when he met up backstage with Bob Dylan at Slane Castle, Ireland, in July 1984. Dylan spoke casually of his love for Irish music — for the Clancy Brothers, the McPeake family, Planxty and Dominic Behan — and extolled the virtues of simple recording as practised in the Fifties and Sixties.

Bono realised that he, an Irishman, knew less about Irish music than the American. He had not even drawn water from the well in his own back yard. "The music of U2 is in space somewhere," he confessed to Dylan. "There is no particular musical roots or heritage for us. In Ireland there is a tradition, but we've never plugged into it."

"Well," Dylan said, "you have to reach back into music. You have to reach back."

Eighteen months later, this time in New York, Bono began his education. Out one night with Peter Wolf, vocalist with the blues-based J. Geils band whom U2 had once supported on tour in America, he was taken down to meet Rolling Stones Mick Jagger and Keith Richards.

Sitting in their room while Richards played country music on the piano and Wolf and Jagger sang some old classics, Bono was again aware of his separation from this tradition. He didn't have the background to join with them — most of the songs were new to him.

U2 in Dublin 1988.

"Then we all went into this room and played a few records," he remembers. "It was a recording by John Lee Hooker that made me realise there was something about the blues that I felt close to, a kind of raw power. When I started listening to Robert Johnson, it was the words that got through to me. I thought 'I can write these words'."

John Lee Hooker came from Clarksdale, Mississippi, lived in Memphis and moved on up to Detroit where he developed a tough urban blues sound. In the clubs he played with a four piece band but on record, starting in 1948, he stuck with an electric guitar and stomped out the beat with his foot. "I was struck by this sound of his boot banging on the floor to keep time," says Bono, "and his voice sounded like razor blades."

That night Bono sat and wrote *Silver and Gold*, a chilling hard-edged song of ropes, guns, shackles and chains, written from the perspective of an unjustly imprisoned South African black. The next day he went into the studio with Keith Richards and Ronnie Wood of the Rolling Stones and cut a version which went out on the *Sun City* album in aid of Artists United Against Apartheid.

Silver and Gold wasn't a blues song as such, but it drew from the harsh elemental imagery familiar in those black country songs from the Mississippi Delta or the city songs of Chicago.

Another long-term inspiration for U2 was John Lennon. In the aftermath of The Beatles, ending a period when he had been hailed as the leader of his generation, he recorded an album, *Plastic Ono Band*, in which he

John Lee Hooker.

Silver & Gold
In the shit house, a shotgun
Praying hands hold me down
If only the hunter was hunted
In this tin can town
No stars in the black night
Looks like the sky fall down
No sun in the daylight
Looks like it's chained to the ground
Broken back to the ceiling
Broken nose to the floor
I scream at the silence
That crawls under the door (under the floor)

Warden says the exit is sold
If you want a way out - Silver & Gold
           - Silver & Gold

There's a rope around my neck
There's a trigger in your gun
Jesus! say something
I am someone

I seen the coming and going the captains and the kings
Their navy blue uniform
Them bright and shiny things
Captains and kings in the slave ships hold
They came to collect
Silver & Gold
Silver & Gold

The temperature is rising
The fever white hot
Mister I ain't got nothing
But it's more than you got

These chains no longer bind me
Nor the shackles at my feet
Outside are the prisoners
Inside the free
Set them free

A prize fighter in the corner is told
Hit where it hurts - Silver & Gold
            - Silver & Gold

You can stop the world from turning around
You just gotta pay a penny in the pound

Written by Bono, Published by Blue Mountain Music (UK) and Chappell Warner Music (ROW).

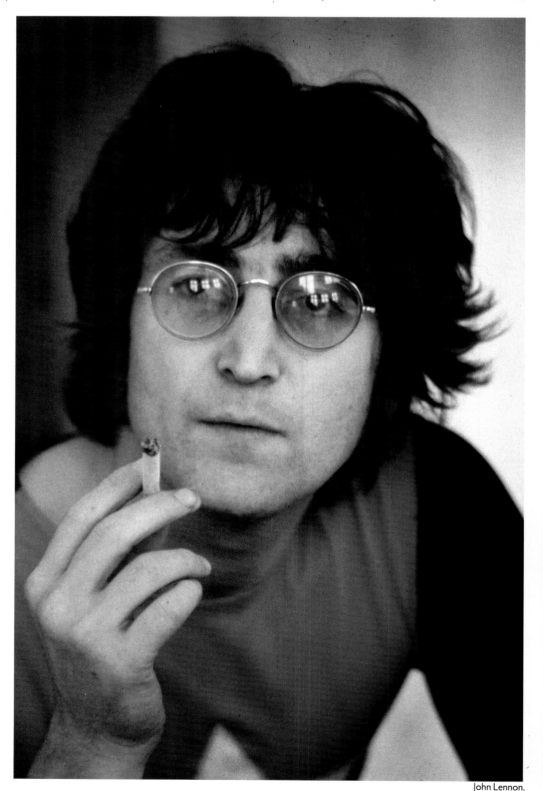

John Lennon.

deliberately revealed himself as a flawed human being with scars going back to his childhood.

"They were blues songs really," says Bono. "They were really stripped to the bone. People get trapped by their roles, by the way they see themselves and the way other people see them. I love the way John Lennon stripped all that away. Sometimes it's O.K. to just look in the mirror and not like what you see."

Also around this time, the other members of U2 were beginning to be attracted to the country songs of Willie Nelson and Johnny Cash, the dust-bowl folk of Woody Guthrie and the gospel of Mahalia Jackson. Discovering this music by playing with the dials on their hotel radios provided an antidote to the faked emotions of soap opera, Madison Avenue and easy listening rock & roll.

In contrast this seemed like rooted music. It reminded them of the Irish music which had been there in the background as they grew up in Dublin and it reminded them that they were not really a part of this limousine-luxury hotel-private jet world of touring.

There is a side to Irish people which relates to the pain of slavery, racism and oppression. "As an Irishman I have a right to be plugged into American music," announced Bono one night on the *Joshua Tree* tour. "A lot of it came from Ireland and crossed the Atlantic in the pockets and memories of the immigrants. That's where folk music came from. English and Scottish music went into it too, but there happened to be a lot more Irish because they were dying of starvation and the country was

Dublin.

so screwed up it couldn't offer them jobs."

U2 had toyed with Irish music on their *October* album by adding oillean pipes and bodhran to one track as an assertion of their nationality, but it had never been taken further. Now they were starting to take tapes of Clannad and Christy Moore on the road with them and to investigate the works of Makem and Clancy.

"When we're away from home that sort of music really gives me some basis for normality," says Adam. "These were the sort of guys you could see singing in Dublin pubs any night of the week. I get a lot of comfort from it because it brings you back to where you belong. Country, blues and reggae have a similar effect for me.

"If you spend any time in America you get sick of the hard sell attitude, and that includes most music on the radio. A lot of the music's got nothing in common with the great American rock & roll. It's just gloss, production line work.

"That's O.K. if that's what those bands are into. They freely admit to the fact that they just want to make a living and that's fair enough, but I don't think that's where we're from."

And so, on the *Joshua Tree* tour, U2 found themselves promoting their past while investigating their future. On stage they played their greatest hits plus almost all of the *Joshua Tree*

album, whilst in hotel rooms they started work on a new set of songs that reflected their new appetite for roots music.

In Memphis the band visited Graceland, Elvis Presley's mansion, and then sat on the banks of the Mississippi, inspiration for so many songs. In Los Angeles they began songwriting with Bob Dylan, writing *Prisoner of Love* and *Love Rescue Me*. In Nashville they were joined on stage by Wynnona Judd, one half of The Judds. In London U2 met Roy Orbison for the first time and played him some of the half-finished country songs they'd been working on. This led to the writing of a new song for Orbison, titled *She's a Mystery to Me*.

The new songs began to pile up. Regine

Moylett, press officer for the tour, remembers The Edge composing one song in a hotel elevator and Bono writing lyrics on a beer mat in a Miami bar and then walking away without them. (He returned later and fished his Art out of a trash can.)

"My songwriting went into overdrive on the tour," admits The Edge. "Now we're working on acoustic guitars rather than improvising, we can write in hotel rooms. I must have ended up with over fifteen new musical ideas. That's been a big change for me."

It would be wrong to portray the *Joshua Tree* tour as a time when U2 forsook their easily identifiable sound for blues, gospel and country. The influence of these types of music — and they will all admit a shallow knowledge of them at present — has been more in terms of inspirational attitude than chord sequences, instrumentation or style.

As Bono says, "It's more the spirit than the flesh of it that has affected us. We're not blues or country aficionados. We are irreverant in our use of it. We're not going to let it in to the point where it takes over and we lose what we are. If we do a blues it will be our type of blues."

Hearing the migrant worker songs of Woody Guthrie, the love torn ballads of Hank Williams and the chilling blues of Robert Johnson took them to the heart of an America they always hoped truly existed behind the billboard signs and mega hype of what writer Martin Amis called 'The Moronic Inferno'.

"It's the spirit of all this music that's affecting us," agrees The Edge. "There's no way we're turning into a revivalist band. Gospel music has strongly affected me. It's exactly the opposite of what modern music is about. Modern music is hiding. It's all stance and image. Gospel to me is total abandon, and that is the beginning of soul.

"I flick on a gospel station in L.A. and hear these black preachers who preach like Aretha Franklin sings. There's more soul in one of these guy's sermons than anything you'd hear on FM radio at the moment. It connects and means something to me."

Speaking of their country music experience of Nashville, Adam says, "We got a vibe off these people that was so much more where we were coming from. If you like, it was kind of Irish. There was none of this slick music business stuff which is often more about business than music.

"We discovered a common bond between us and some of these older artists like B.B. King. When we met him there was a whole world of understanding and nothing needed to be said. That has been the pay-off of working ten years to get into this position. We no longer have to prove ourselves. It's in the music and people can hear it."

U2 and . B.B. King in Fort Worth, Texas.

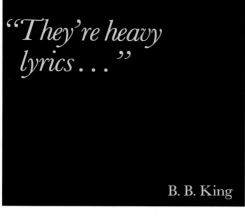

"They're heavy lyrics . . . "

B. B. King

Meeting veteran blues player B. B. King, a Memphis man whose recording career began before Elvis's, provided another opportunity to experiment with the blues.

The relationship between B.B. King and U2 began in Dublin back in the early part of 1986. They met up whilst B.B. King was working in Ireland, and had talked about doing some writing and recording together at some unspecified point in the future.

The band wrote *When Love Comes to Town* for him, Bono only finishing the lyrics an hour before he met him in Fort Worth, Texas. B.B.'s response after reading the paper Bono had given him was to say "How old are you? They're heavy lyrics . . . heavy lyrics."

"Seeing him that close was great," says The Edge, newly an admirer of blues guitarists from Howlin' Wolf to Jimi Hendrix. "I loved his style and it was good to meet the man."

B.B. and his band opened for U2 in Texas, which U2 looked upon as a great honour. The sequence in the movie was filmed during soundcheck and the gig at the Tarrant County Arena in Fort Worth, and on this one occasion only *When Love Comes to Town* was performed live by the two bands as a special encore.

"We discovered a common bond between us and some of these older artists like B. B. King. When we met him there was a whole world of understanding and nothing needed to be said. That has been the pay-off of working ten years to get into this position. We no longer have to prove ourselves. It's in the music and people can hear it."

Adam.

When Love Comes to Town

> *"We waited to find a film-maker who seemed to understand what U2 were trying to do."*
>
> Paul McGuinness

Why a U2 movie? Paul McGuinness, U2's manager, explains. "It came about for a number of reasons but one of the main ones was to kill Red Rocks, which was made in 1983 and now looks very dated. The music that U2 perform now is not represented, yet it's still in the top ten video sales charts after five years."

The video *Under a Blood Red Sky* was extremely successful in capturing the energy of U2 live on top of a mountain in the pouring rain back in 1983, which probably explains why it still sells so well. All the same, the band felt it was time to move on, and let Red Rocks

become a piece of history, rather than still be used to represent U2 now. "Every time someone on television wants to show U2 live," continues McGuinness, "you always get these four rather shiny-faced adolescents clambering about. It really has to be replaced. We also felt that there was a film to be made which would be good enough for people to go to the cinemas to see. The terrible thing about television is that you still only hear the sound through a tiny little speaker. That's always a disappointment — whatever the pictures are like the sound is always appalling on T.V."

One of the first major decisions was the

Paul McGuinness.

Why a U2 movie?

choice of a director for the film. Having quietly let it be known that there could be a U2 movie in the offing, the band began to follow up various possibilities. The choice proved to be difficult. "A lot of major name directors wanted to do it," says McGuinness, "we met with a number of them, but we were waiting to meet somebody who seemed to be on our wavelength and had strong ideas of his own about how the film should be made. We didn't start out with a script and say 'who's going to make this film?', we waited to find a film-maker who seemed to understand what U2 were trying to do musically and on stage. That's why we chose Phil Joanou."

In film directing circles, the name Phil Joanou is still a new one. Joanou was only 25 years old when he was hired by U2, and had previously made only one feature film, a teen comedy called *Three O'Clock High*. He was given an introduction to the band by John Sykes, an old friend of Paul McGuinness from the early days of M.T.V. John had subsequently gone to work at the major Hollywood agency C.A.A. and introduced several of the directors that the band were interested in meeting. This meeting culminated in Phil Joanou's arrival on the tour one night in Hartford, Connecticut.

The band were on tour in Europe when

ideas began to formulate for the movie's structure, and the details started to become clearer. There would be three kinds of footage in the film — concert footage in colour and in black & white, plus documentary footage in 16mm black & white. U2 would finance the making of the movie themselves, hoping to make the necessary deals at a later stage.

The first parts of the film to be shot were some of the documentary sections. With the rough structure decided, a small film-crew arrived almost immediately. By this time the *Joshua Tree* tour had found its way back to the USA, and the filming commenced. There were just two cameras in the "documentary crew", one operated by Joanou himself, the other by the director of photography, Robert Brinkmann. For the next few months, these two cameras followed Bono, Edge, Adam and Larry everywhere, and the band were generally patient enough to put up with the intrusion.

By the end of the tour there had been easily enough footage shot to make several complete documentary films without needing a single inch of live film. Consequently, when it came to selecting sequences to go into the finished movie there were some tough decisions to be made. In the end U2 and Joanou selected the parts they felt were the most interesting, and fitted best with the structure of the movie as a whole.

Director Phil Joanou.

Phil Joanou
DIRECTOR

Native of Los Angeles, California, Joanou studied at the theatre school of UCLA and subsequently went on to graduate from USC film school. On the strength of his graduation film, he directed two episodes of Steven Spielberg's *Amazing Stories,* and later began work at the Amblin company in Hollywood. Joanou went on to direct *Three O'Clock High* in 1986, immediately followed by *U2: Rattle & Hum* in 1987, which he also edited.

Michael Hamlyn
PRODUCER

Started work as an Assistant Director in London in the 70's. Formed Midnight Films in 1981 to produce *The Secret Policeman's Other Ball.*

For the last six years he has worked with directors such as Julien Temple, Meiert Avis and Richard Lowenstein on film and music related projects, including music clips for The Rolling Stones, The Kinks, Pete Townshend, U2, Sade, INXS and Bruce Springsteen.

"Michael was nearly dragged off to jail by the Los Angeles Police Department during the making of the *Where The Streets Have No Name* video. That's the kind of producer we were looking for" says Paul McGuinness.

Paul McGuinness
EXECUTIVE PRODUCER

Despite being known as the manager of U2, Paul McGuinness also has a grounding in film making. He started his career as a film production manager and assistant director in television commercials.

In 1978 he abandoned movies to take on full time management of U2, on the premise that "I could have been wrong, but I only had to be right once."

Over the past ten years McGuinness has been a fundamental part of U2's success, taking care of the band's business, whilst remaining their advisor, critic and friend.

"Stop The Traffic – Rock & Roll."

Bono (Graffiti)

Over twenty years ago, during the "Summer of Love", the Bay Area gave birth to a new music scene. It was the era of tie-dye T-shirts, The Grateful Dead, peace, love and free festivals.

This city of Sixties revolution has always been a source of fascination for U2. As a tribute to the city, in the spirit of years gone by, the band decided to hold their own free gig. It really was a spur of the moment decision. The band were in San Francisco, but the entire roadcrew and all the equipment had already arrived in Vancouver to set up for the next show a couple of days later. The band were not going to let this be a problem. Without a single item of their own equipment, just a handful of the crew and a sound system borrowed from The Grateful Dead, U2 set up and played on the back of a truck in front of a huge fountain sculpture in an open space down by the Embarcadero.

The office workers on lunch-break from the financial district couldn't believe their luck. Being the week after the first major stock-

San Francisco, California.

market crash of the year, Bono dubbed the free concert a "save the yuppies" benefit, and invited donations of briefcases.

The band opened with Dylan's *All Along the Watchtower,* despite the fact that they didn't actually know how to play it. Within minutes the square was jammed with a crowd of around 20,000 and traffic came to a standstill on the overpass that runs behind the area.

Then came Bono's much publicised graffiti episode. The singer climbed the fountain sculpture, a grey concrete cage, to spray "Stop the traffic — Rock & Roll".

The mayor of the town was less than happy and immediately put out a warrant for Bono's arrest. However, after several attempts to apprehend Bono, and a couple of weeks' legal wrangling, all parties eventually agreed that the whole thing was not worth the argument — particularly as the graffiti had been cleaned off the following day.

Bono now blames the incident on tour madness, though the timing was fortuitous. The mayor of San Francisco at the time was Diane Feinstein. In an attempt to sanction graffiti art in the city she had offered $500

bounty for anyone bringing graffiti artists in to custody.

The Mission district of San Francisco contains some of the world's finest mural and graffiti art, so naturally this edict from City Hall caused outrage amongst the local artists' community.

However, shortly after U2's free gig, a new mayor, Art Agnos, was elected. He decided to abolish the bounty and use this same money to set up a fund sponsoring the work of graffiti artists in the city.

All Along the Watchtower
By Bob Dylan

"There must be some way out of here," said the joker to the thief,
"There's too much confusion, I can't get no relief.
Businessmen, they drink my wine, plowmen dig my earth,
None of them along the line know what any of it is worth."

"No reason to get excited," the thief, he kindly spoke,
"There are many here among us who feel that life is but a joke.
But you and I, we've been through that, and this is not our fate,
So let us not talk falsely now, the hour is getting late."

All along the watchtower, princes kept the view
While all the women came and went, barefoot servants, too.

Outside in the distance a wildcat did growl,
Two riders were approaching, the wind began to howl.

© 1968 DWARF MUSIC
All Rights Reserved. International Copyright Secured.
Reprinted by Permission.

> *"A gospel song with a restless spirit."*
>
> Bono.

A church in New York's Harlem has a choir who call themselves "The New Voices of Freedom." The band heard about them via a tape which the choir had sent to Island records in New York—a recording of their own version of U2's *Still Haven't Found What I'm Looking For*. During the live shows Bono had often introduced this song as "… kind of a gospel song with a restless spirit", and this tape was a confirmation of that. The band were so taken with the choir's gospel version of their song, that they got in touch with the church and paid a visit. Harlem is the old capital of Black New York. U2 hadn't been there before, so with Gavin Friday, a friend from Dublin, they spent a little time checking out the area before meeting up with the choir.

U2 accompanied by a gospel choir seems an unlikely combination. For the U2 of *Boy* or *War* it would have seemed absurd, but *Still Haven't Found* had never sounded so joyful. Bono sang the melody, with his arm still in a sling from an on-stage tumble the previous week, The Edge played quiet guitar and "The New Voices of Freedom" did the rest. It worked so beautifully that a few days later at Bono's request, the whole choir joined U2 on stage at Madison Square Garden.

Gavin Friday with Bono.

Harlem, New York

Bono and the Million Dollar Quartet (Jerry Lee Lewis, Carl Perkins, Elvis Presley, Johnny Cash).

> *"It was like – throw out technology."*
>
> Adam

In 1941, Sam C. Phillips dropped out of high school in his home town of Florence, Alabama. His father had died and he needed to support his mother, but continued to study at night school. He majored in engineering, but also took delightfully obscure minor courses in podiatry and embalming. Following his interest in music, but being a self-confessed non-musician, he became a radio D.J., firstly in Alabama and then in Nashville before moving to Memphis in 1945 where he eventually got a job with the radio station WREC.

By 1950 he had acquired enough capital to open a small studio at 706 Union Ave., Memphis, and began to make recordings of local artists. Initially he obtained releases by licensing through the successful Chess label in Chicago, and the Modern label in Los Angeles. To help make ends meet, he would also make less glamorous recordings, such as weddings or club meetings, which would be recorded onto a single sided L.P. Success followed quickly and Sam Phillips began to make his mark in the embryonic music industry of the time. As time went on, however, Chess began to lose confidence in Phillips' choice of new artists. When he

Sun Studio, Memphis

wanted to concentrate on recording black artists, there were few people who would take him seriously.

Consequently in 1952, aided by his brother Judd, he set up his own label — Sun Records — and in his own words, Phillips "never fooled with anybody who had ever recorded before I found them."

Sun was one of a number of new independent record labels in the southern United States which flourished in the post-war period, making the most of the budding jazz, blues and hillbilly markets.

Phillips' most famous discovery occurred when he went in search of "a white guy that could sing like a black guy". The guy he found was Elvis Presley. Although Elvis was not to stay with Sun Records for very long, Phillips launched his career, and introduced the young Presley to the recording studio — Sun Studio.

In the years that followed, the list of legends who recorded at Sun is too long to recount, but just a few of the greats include Jerry Lee Lewis, Johnny Cash, Roy Orbison and Carl Perkins.

Thirty years later, U2 arrived at Sun Studio, which is now owned and run by Gary Hardy. With all its history and so much atmosphere, the band considered it a privilege to visit the premises, let alone use the studio. It was something of a symbolic return to the roots of rock & roll, to the place where rock & roll was invented.

In the control room was 'Cowboy' Jack Clement, formerly technical assistant to Sam

Roy Orbison.

The Edge observed by Phil Joanou.

Phillips. Clement had been in this same room when Jerry Lee Lewis, born and raised in the Assembly of God church and a cousin of T.V. preacher Jimmy Swaggart, had suffered a stricken conscience over recording *Great Balls Of Fire,* holding up the session while he denounced rock & roll as 'worldly music' and claimed that he had the Devil in him. Now Clement was here engineering a version of Woody Guthrie's *Jesus Christ* for a band with a core of believers.

U2 also cut *When Love Comes to Town, Little Angel of Harlem, She's a Mystery to Me* and a U2/Dylan collaboration, *Love Rescue Me,* hoping to benefit not just from the history of the room but the basic recording set up.

Since *The Unforgettable Fire,* recorded at Slane Castle in Dublin with Brian Eno and Daniel Lanois, they'd been going for as live a sound as possible, avoiding unnecessary overdubs, and Sun Studio offered a further step in the direction of simplicity.

"It was like — throw out technology," recalls Adam. "Give us a microphone and a bit of tape and you do the bit in between."

At this point in time, U2 were perhaps at their closest to a musical style which Sam Phillips would recognise, but Phillips' statement about his own success is one the band would hope to echo during their whole career: "Rock & roll music has a very favourable impact on the understanding among races. The young are not so prejudiced as the old, and if I've done something to stop the prejudice growing up, then I think I've done something."

> *"I don't know whether U2 were more excited to be at Sun, or if we were more excited to have them here."*
>
> Gary Hardy, owner of Sun Studio

After U2's session at Sun, a local magazine *The Memphis Star* published this article, written by Dawn Baldwin. It gives an account of the band's visit seen from the other side of the studio door.

Early October. Gary Hardy, Sun's owner, receives a call from Greg McCarthy, who says he is with A & M Records. He asks about studio time for a full day early in November and says he has an artist who wants to get an authentic Rockabilly sound.

"I was a little suspicious at first, but I knew that Greg was Jimmy Iovine's assistant," says Gary. "But I didn't make any connection at first. A & M is not U2's label and besides, this was all out of the blue."

About a week later, he gets a call from 'Cowboy' Jack Clement, who was the engineer at Sun in the late Fifties, when the Million Dollar Quartet was at its prime, and has more recently produced material for Johnny Cash. Jack asks, "Have these guys from U2 got a hold of you?" but he isn't exactly sure who they are. For Gary, however, the pieces of the mystery are beginning to come together and his excitement builds.

Once Gary has confirmed that U2 is coming, he, Sun engineer David Aron, and

The Memphis Star

Gary Hardy with Bono and The Edge.

Jack begin doing a little research on the band and talking to Jimmy Iovine, finding out what kind of equipment they need to have on hand. But fancy electronic gadgets and remote recording units aren't on the list.

"Basically, U2 record like they used to record here," Gary explains. "They set up as a band and they record everything live at the same time. They don't use headphones. They wanted to come here for the magic of the room. The only effect they wanted was that unique tape slap-back echo off the studio floor."

But as the session date draws near, they discover a few odds and ends they need. "Chips (Moman) was very helpful in lending us mikes and baffles and Ardent provided a digital two-track machine when Jimmy Iovine finally got around to mentioning that they wanted a digital two-track live master

from the session," says Gary. "There were a lot of last minute phone calls."

Jack Clement and his engineer David Ferguson come into town a day early to check out the studio. They determine that everything is ready to go.

Film crews arrive at the studio and begin setting up to film the session.

The band arrives that Sunday night under a veil of secrecy. Gary and David, as instructed, have managed to keep the whole event under wraps. Still, the rumour mills are churning as studio hands and musicians throughout the city speculate about what's going on at Sun.

The morning of the session, Bono and the boys are out at Graceland, shooting additional film footage.

According to Gary, as Bono walks through the trophy room, he stops in front of a gold

Sun record and says. "There would be no U2, there would have been no Elvis, if there hadn't been a Sun."

"I really don't know if they were more excited to be here or if we were more excited to have them," says Gary. "It was close."

Then, at noon, while the band is still at Graceland, Jimmy Iovine calls from New York and says he needs three female backup singers. Can Gary get them by that afternoon at 3 pm? "I tell him sure, no problem and call up Phyllis and Helen Duncan and Becky Evans (of Reba and the Portables) and have them on stand-by although they have no idea what it's for.

Three o'clock comes, then four, then five. Jimmy Iovine arrives. The film crew is ready. All preproduction has been taken care of. Everyone sits and waits for the band. Then the phone rings. None of the band members have

instruments.

"So Dennis Sheehan, the tour manager, gives me a list of everything they need and I start calling Charlie Lawing at Strings and Things and different studios trying to find all the best equipment," says Gary. "And in the end there were a few things I couldn't find that I was especially concerned about. One of them was a snare for Larry. But when the band got here about 7.30 pm, it turned out it didn't matter anyway.

"They stopped outside and read the plaque and then came in, made introductions, and immediately began running to the vintage instruments that I have bought to go with the studio. The drum kit, a '53 Telecaster and a '54 Gibson ES295 and an old Fender amp. We had all these thousand-dollar microphones in here and Bono used the old WHBQ microphone that Dewey Phillips used

in his broadcasts," Gary laughs, obviously incredulous.

It isn't until U2 actually arrives, that Gary and David find out that they have come to Sun specifically for the purpose of recording *When They Lay Jesus Christ In His Grave* for a Woody Guthrie memorial album in collaboration with several other artists.

But once the band gets into the groove of being in Sun Studio with the vintage instruments and the pictures of Elvis and Jerry Lee on the walls, and all those spirits floating around the room, the Guthrie song turns into a spine-tingling, foot-stomping, hair-raising spiritual they like so much they decide to record three more songs and end up staying until 3 am. Well over an hour of mastered material is produced at the session.

On one rockabilly song they decide they need someone to play piano, so Gary calls

around for Tony Thomas of the Bluebeats. "I found him over at Cotton Row in the middle of a session but he, well, acquiesed to join us and played the old Wurlitzer and a B3 organ," says Gary. "And the Duncan Sisters and Becky were really an absolute inspiration."

Gary smiles as he strolls around the studio, breathing deeply, as if to soak up a little more of the magic energy only Sun can create.

"These guys loved it. They loved everything. I mean they are very, very real people, no pretensions about themselves or others. They're artists. And for them and for all of us, this was a true historic happening. This room brings it out in people. No one can take credit for it. It's just here.

"And I'm really not exaggerating", he adds, "when I tell you they didn't want to leave."

Reprinted by kind permission of the Memphis Star magazine, © December 1987.

Phyllis and Helen Duncan and Becky Evans.

"In this movie there's no such word as 'Cut'."

Steve Iredale, Production Manager

One of the central motivations for U2 making a movie was simply to record U2 live on the *Joshua Tree* tour. It was this tour which had established them as what *Rolling Stone* called "the most influential rock band of the Eighties", and it was important for the film to show just how it had been. As there were both indoor and outdoor shows on the tour, the band decided to film both. Eventually a decision was made to film the indoor concerts in black & white, and the outdoor gigs in colour. This would prove a bigger task than was first anticipated.

For a band on stage, cameras create a completely different atmosphere in which to perform. Especially for a band like U2, for whom two-way communication with the audience is vital, the addition of cameras becomes a problem. There's the immediate physical presence to deal with — U2 have never felt comfortable performing with cameras right in front of their faces. And for Bono there is the particular worry that the audience may feel relegated to second place, that they have just been brought in to make up the numbers.

For the U2 organisation, the filming came as quite a shock to the system. Having been out on the road all year, the touring party (including the band) had a regular routine and the whole operation running extremely smoothly. The invasion of the film crew was

U2 Live on Film

very disruptive, and everyone was forced to adjust to new requirements.

There were countless technical details to be arranged. U2's live sound engineer, Joe O'Herlihy, had to deal with the presence of Jimmy Iovine's mobile recording studio and split feeds had to be arranged from the 74 onstage audio channels, to pass signals to Joe outfront and Jimmy in the mobile. Peter Williams, U2's lighting director, worked with the directors of photography to bring together the filming and the live show. U2's on stage crew found themselves with an assault course of camera tracks, operators and cables to work around.

Any technical problems were compounded by the fact that, generally, there is very little crossover between the film and rock & roll industries. Their ways of working are very different. On a rock & roll tour, the whole entourage is constantly setting up, taking down and moving on. Everything has to be ready for when the doors open, so in the running of the day things have to happen *now!* This requires a swift mode of operation, but one often seen by film-makers as sloppy and haphazard.

On the other hand, filming is a very expensive process, so there can be no room for mistakes once cameras are rolling. Strict attention is given to the most minute detail, because when magnified onto a huge cinema screen small mistakes become glaring errors. Consequently, a film shoot is characterised by meticulous care over technical specifications, and the constant "stop-start" nature of the day's work. Compared to the pace of a rock & roll tour, this approach can seem pedantic, not to mention crushingly slow.

Film making is about creating mood and atmosphere for the camera's eye, and anything beyond the edges of the screen is totally irrelevant. Rock & roll is about a total production for a live audience. Fusing the two methods of working was not going to be easy, and the concert film-shoots, both black & white and colour, each presented unique challenges.

Filming at the Sun Devils Stadium.

Ellen Darst
PRINCIPLE MANAGEMENT, NEW YORK

U2's side of the liaison between key film personnel, companies and crews was handled by Ellen Darst.

Ellen is a director of Principle Management and runs the New York office.

She has been involved with U2 ever since the band first came to America on the *Boy* tour in 1980, originally whilst working in artist development at Warner Brothers who at that time were the U.S. distributors for Island Records.

Ellen left Warner Brothers in 1982 and began full-time work with U2 in early 1983.

Jimmy Iovine
MUSIC PRODUCER

Jimmy Iovine was producer for the live soundtrack of *U2: Rattle & Hum*. He is by no means inexperienced in working with U2's live music having produced the live mini-LP *Under a Blood Red Sky* in 1983, and several other more recent recordings including *Baby Please Come Home* for the Special Olympics Christmas album in 1987. During the editing of the film, Iovine worked with U2 in Los Angeles to produce the movie soundtrack as well as the live and new studio tracks for the *Rattle & Hum* album.

Joe O'Herlihy
LIVE SOUND ENGINEER

Having taken care of U2's live sound since 1978, there are only a handful of U2 shows at which Joe O'Herlihy has not been present. He has worked with the band from the smallest club dates right up to the Joshua Tree stadium shows which utilised the most powerful sound system ever put together in Europe.

Whilst touring O'Herlihy was also responsible for co-ordinating the live recordings made at various venues around the world, with producers Jimmy Iovine and Steve Lillywhite.

"We had no second chances – it all had to work first time."

Gregg Fienberg, Associate Producer.

Chicago had been the original choice of location for the black & white film shoot. This was partly because of the great Chicago audience, but mostly because it was the only city on the tour in which U2 played three indoor shows. However, the Chicago venue was found to be unsuitable for filming, so the production team began searching for other possibilities. The McNichols Arena in Denver, Colorado, presented itself as ideal, so the choice became obvious. The band were more than happy to film here, recalling very positive memories of making the Red Rocks video in 1983.

The black & white filming was done using eight cameras; two on platforms in the audience, three on dolly-tracks across the front and side of the stage, one Louma Crane (a camera on a mobile boom-arm) on a dolly-track behind the stage, one camera taking a constant wide-shot from the back of the venue and one mobile operator with a hand-held camera.

Director of photography for the black & white shoot was Robert Brinkmann. He had worked with director Phil Joanou previously, and was also the director of photography for the black & white documentary footage.

U2 in Black & White

Denver: Quiet Before the Storm.

Brinkmann had been on the *Joshua Tree* tour with the documentary crew for a couple of months prior to Denver, which gave him an opportunity to get used to the somewhat unorthodox way that U2 work. This was an advantage that most of the Denver film crew did not share.

It has to be said that the whole event was staggeringly under-rehearsed. The film shoot had to fit into the exacting tour schedule, and there were only two shows in Denver, preceded by a day off. The free day enabled transport of the touring equipment to Denver from St. Paul, Minneapolis, where the previous show had been. But owing to a basketball game at McNichols Arena, access to the venue wasn't permitted until midnight before the first show.

This left only 18 hours to set up the entire complement of film equipment, camera tracks, install the mobile recording studio, set lighting levels and have a limited rehearsal so that the band and cameramen would have some idea of what to expect on the night.

Events were more than a little rushed, but most of the necessary equipment was up and running by the time doors opened at 6.30 pm. The opening act, The BoDeans, played their set to a rowdy audience, whilst trying to ignore technicians still setting up final pieces of film equipment.

When U2 eventually took to the stage, they found themselves on decidedly unfamiliar territory. Everything seemed different to their regular show. It looked different, it sounded different and there was the added pressure of knowing this show would be recorded on film. Bono was losing confidence and sensed the crowd could feel it. This was not going to be a great show. After months of bringing down the house on a nightly basis, the cameras had arrived. Anger and frustration drove Bono through the rest of the night, and some of the movie's most intense parts of the black & white footage were the result.

However, film director Phil Joanou was far from despairing. Crowding around a video

monitor in the dressing room after the show, he and the band watched a playback of the snowy images from which the film cameras "video tap", a device which allows images on film stock to be video taped. The pictures are of very poor quality, but at least give a general idea of what was going on.

Phil was very enthusiastic about the work of some of the camera operators, particularly on the Louma Crane. Even in the face of an uncertain band, Phil was characteristically animated, and several hours of video tape later, even Bono was beginning to realise things weren't nearly as bad as he'd imagined. It actually wasn't very different from a regular show, it had just felt like it.

The second night was a declaration of war. The technicians had all day to make adjustments and the band had time for a proper soundcheck. Everyone felt far more prepared, and it showed. From the opening *Streets* to the closing song *"40"*, the band, the audience and the technicians put on a great performance.

Back in the dressing room after the show there was a mixture of excitement and relief. It was champagne all round and more viewing of the video playback. Everyone swapped stories of how their night had been and how it looked from their point of view — Bono said he knew he was onto a winner when he could see the cameramen trying to dance.

As often happens with U2, the spontaneity

of filming made for the best results. It was most gratifying to have fitted this film shoot into the touring schedule and seen it work, but everyone was aware that the full colour film shoot outdoors in Arizona was going to be on a much bigger scale.

Jordan Cronenweth A.S.C.

DIRECTOR OF PHOTOGRAPHY
(Colour)

Cronenweth is a highly respected director of photography with an impressive track record. His career goes back as far as *Butch Cassidy and the Sundance Kid* and includes *Bladerunner, Stop Making Sense, Altered States* and *Peggy Sue Got Married*. He was responsible for the cinematography of the colour concert footage in *U2: Rattle & Hum* shot at Tempe, Arizona.

Peter Williams

LIGHTING DESIGNER

Peter Williams, generally known as "Willie", has been U2's Lighting Designer/Director for over six years and is the token Englishman on the U2 crew.

For both the concert shoots he worked closely with the directors of photography to capture on film the atmosphere of U2 live, operating the lighting system during the shows and giving cues to up to thirty followspot operators.

Robert Brinkmann

DIRECTOR OF PHOTOGRAPHY
(Black & White)

Originally from Berlin, Brinkmann studied and graduated with Phil Joanou at University of Southern California. He worked on Joanou's graduation film.

Brinkmann was director of photography at the Denver concert shoot as well as being director of photography/camera operator for the documentary footage, and camera operator at the Arizona concert.

Steve Iredale

U2 PRODUCTION MANAGER

From Co. Mayo in the West of Ireland, Steve Iredale is another long-term member of the U2 crew.

He is responsible for the mechanics of organising the entire touring unit, ensuring that all the various departments of the operation come together.

During the filming of *Rattle & Hum* Iredale was in constant liaison with the Midnight Films production team to integrate the filming schedule into the existing structure of the tour.

"It was like Apocalypse Now without so many helicopters."

Bono

U2's concert film shoot in Tempe, Arizona, was an unprecedented task, described by Bono as "like *Apocalypse Now*, without so many helicopters". There have been many other concert movies, of course, some of them quite brilliant, but none has attempted to capture on film a show of this scale after dark. As well as the stage, there was the entire stadium and the massive crowd to be lit to make good for the cameras.

The film's associate producer, Gregg Fienberg, explains: "We had over $100,000 of lighting and grip equipment. That was the total for all the rental gear and the pieces we had to buy, just for lighting, that's not including cameras, personnel or anything. Usually that budget would do a whole feature film — we spent that much in a week. Colin Campbell (gaffer for the Arizona shoot) said he thought it was the biggest cinematic lighting achievement ever, based on the fact that we had to light 70,000 people, get light levels on them all, plus of course a 200 ft. x 80 ft. stage. I mean, it was a different operation to making an epic, like *Ben Hur* or something. You look at a film like, say *The Mission*, where you have these rigs which the grips build through trees and camera tracks over cliffs and

Raving Arizona

so on — its a different sort of rigging, but in terms of lighting an event Arizona was a very big deal. It was so elaborate and we had no second chances — it all had to work first time.''

By choosing to make a film of this type U2 knew they were taking a huge risk; filming outdoors at night with a live audience and no second chances if anything were to go wrong.

To add to this pressure, there was the weather. The *Under a Blood Red Sky* video is testimony to the meteorological curse under which U2 live. Arizona was much the same.

U2's gigantic outdoor stage was loaded into the stadium a week before the shoot to give time for assembly and four complete days for setting up, camera run-throughs and so on.

It rained. It rained pretty consistently from the arrival of the first scaffolding truck to the arrival of the last member of the audience. Arizona is largely desert, yet U2 still managed to produce a full week of rain.

There was, however, another problem which no-one had anticipated. With this being the first film of its kind, it became obvious that there were no 'experts' to consult for advice. Many of the people working on the film crew were the best in their respective fields, but when it came to the outdoor shoot, no-one had worked on anything quite like it before.

The director of photography for the colour concert footage was Jordan Cronenweth, A.S.C., highly acclaimed within the film industry for his work on such visual master-pieces as *Bladerunner, Altered States* and *Stop Making Sense*. He and his film crew are at the top of their profession, but the spontaneous nature of this film, the working conditions and, more than anything, simply the *speed* with which things had to come together were a whole new experience.

With a regular movie, the director of photography and the film crew might spend many hours getting the lighting correct for one sequence, then shoot several takes of the same five minutes of footage before moving on to the next sequence, perhaps in a different location. With the U2 movie there were just three nights in the rain to prepare the entire show.

This gave the crew very little opportunity

to get to know the show and the rather un-usual way in which U2 work. Many of the film crew did not even have the chance to stop and recognise the songs in the live set. This proved very confusing when it came to giving cues for specific numbers — particularly as the band have a habit of changing the set list mid-show. A compromise was worked out which involved members of U2's own crew wearing labels saying "I know what song this is", so at least the film crew would know who to ask in an emergency.

Despite the drizzle, set-up continued as planned. Staging was built and re-built to accommodate special equipment and camera tracks. Sound and lighting gear came in, and finally the band's own on-stage equipment.

Being an after-dark shoot, most of the settings and run throughs had to be done at night. Four brave stand-ins took the place of Bono, Edge, Adam and Larry to hang about for hours in the freezing rain, whilst technicians took light readings, focus pullers took measurements and camera operators explored various angles.

The night before the first of the two shows to be filmed, the band came in for soundcheck and a complete dress rehearsal. The idea was to have a run-through from start to finish to give everyone a chance to see how it would be on the night. Unfortunately, the minute the band struck up, virtually every inhabitant of the local area came down to see what was going on. With ticket prices for the shows

being only $5.00, much of the audience had travelled in from points all over the USA. Many had arrived in Tempe a day early and were not going to miss out on a minute of the U2 film experience.

Within half an hour the police had stopped the rehearsal. Having thousands of people inside a stadium on the night of a show is one thing, but having thousands of people in the street outside a stadium constitutes a public nuisance.

All that remained now was the show the following day. Once the audience were in the stadium and the show had started, there would be no breaks, no re-runs and no chance for adjustments. As U2's production manager Steve Iredale observed, "in this movie there's

no such word as 'cut'."

B. B. King opened both of the Arizona shows for U2. Despite the cold, his warm music lifted up the huge crowd, as twilight turned into darkness over the stadium. Last minute checks were frantically being undertaken throughout, and in their dressing room the members of U2 were still discussing which arrangement of *Sunday Bloody Sunday* would work best. There was an air of optimism that the raw tension would produce great results, though the over-riding feeling was that another week's rehearsal wouldn't have been a bad idea.

Show time finally arrived. There was a word of introduction from Barry Fey, the Denver promoter and long-term friend of U2,

then the house lights went out. Adam pressed the button to start the sequence for *Where The Streets Have No Name*. The band walked on, as the giant lightning machines on stage let rip with apocalyptic flashes. The song built to the first crash, the stadium lights came on, and there was no going back.

Streets went into *I Will Follow*, with a growing feeling from on-stage that all was not well. Bono had the same feeling he'd had the first night at Denver — the feeling that in front of the cameras, the show just wasn't happening. The only trouble was that this time he was right. A couple of numbers later the crowd was definitely subdued, a little over-awed by the whole film event.

In his control room backstage Phil Joanou

was looking at the video-tape monitors showing him what the cameras were getting. He was no happier than the band. The camera operators just weren't prepared for what was happening. During the freezing rehearsals, the stand-ins had been pretty much motionless, and the band's run-through had been stopped by the police. Even though Phil had tried to explain beforehand that this wasn't going to be a cabaret show, most of the camera operators were just left standing. Joanou was most distressed.

Even amid the panic, though, there were some lighter moments. As a gesture to the uncertain audience, Bono took leave of absence from the set-list and led the band into a completely unscheduled performance of *Out*

of Control. He leapt offstage and down the central camera run into the middle of the stadium — a gesture much appreciated by the crowd. The scheduled song for that moment had been the soft vocal solo *M.L.K.*, which was to be lit by a single light on Bono's face with a giant windmill blade turning in the darkness to break up the beam. The film technician who had been given the task of turning the windmill by hand, had been instructed under pain of death exactly where to stand, what to do and when to do it — during the fifth song.

With Bono in the centre of the stadium, U2 thrashed through *Out of Control* – one of their earliest and rowdiest numbers, with every white light in the stadium on and a crowd roaring at last. Turning to face the stage amid the chaos, Bono spotted the film technician on stage in full view, still faithfully turning his windmill blade, obviously feeling very embarrassed and thinking "this song just wasn't like this at rehearsals, but they said the fifth number . . . ". There he stayed until the end of the number, when the band finally went into *M.L.K.* – and he packed up and left.

By the end of the show, virtually everybody was ready to pack up and leave. It really hadn't been a great show and everybody knew it. Phil Joanou was seething, describing the night as "a total disaster", the band weren't happy and there were emergency meetings being called left, right and centre. Even attempted encouragements like "well, at least we got a dress rehearsal" fell flat. Everyone was despondent — and it was still raining.

The following morning things looked a little brighter, and there was even a little desert sunshine coming through at last. The entire day was spent in discussions and making technical re-arrangements for the show that night. Having a much clearer idea of how it would be gave everyone a better chance to prepare properly. Camera positions were moved, lights were adjusted, settings were changed.

The audience too, would be better prepared for the second night — tickets were so cheap that most people were coming to both shows. The second night's filming was the last show on the nine-month *Joshua Tree*

tour, and Christmas was only five days away, so there was a party atmosphere building by the minute.

Night fell again, and nobody looked back. The band went for the jugular, and all the way down the line the show came together. Cameras moved beautifully, the sound was glorious, the lighting worked, the band played well and the audience responded appropriately. Most of the colour footage in the final cut of the movie came from this night.

Before finally closing with *Mothers of the Disappeared*, Bono toasted the birth of two babies in the U2 family. A girl for sound engineer Joe O'Herlihy and a boy for keyboard technician Des Broadbery — both born that week. By way of celebration and also remembering that everyone could finally go

home the following day, U2 gave a once in a lifetime rendition of *Christmas - Baby Please Come Home*, the Phil Spector classic they recorded for the Special Olympics Christmas album that year.

The night was a victory. The band were delighted, Phil Joanou was beaming and the film's producer's, Michael Hamlyn and Paul McGuinness were looking much relieved. In the dressing room there was celebration all round. Many of U2's family and business partners had flown in to witness the filming and the last show of the mammoth tour, including Chris Blackwell, the head of Island Records who would be releasing the soundtrack. Also present were Sid Ganis and Barry London from Paramount Pictures — having just made the arrangement to be the movie's

distributors and wanting a first-hand look at the film's principle characters — and Bill Prezzano, the general manager of Kodak film.

The band called in the U2 crew for thanks, a few laughs and a few beers — and also Barry Fey who'd had his white sneakers *painted* black to comply with the all-black onstage dress code.

The goodbyes were said, although it would be several days before the last trucks finally departed from the stadium. The touring party headed home, quite literally in all directions across the globe, in the knowledge that there was some great concert footage 'in the can'. All that remained for Phil Joanou was to edit it and make it into a movie.

Mothers of the Disappeared

Midnight, our sons and daughters
Were cut down taken from us
Hear their heartbeat . . .
We hear their heartbeat
In the wind we hear their laughter
In the rain
We see their tears
Hear their heartbeat
We hear their heartbeat

Night hangs like a prisoner
Stretched over black and blue
Hear their heartbeat
We hear their heartbeat
In the trees our sons stand naked
Through the walls
Our daughters cry
See their tears in the rain fall

Written by U2, Published by Blue Mountain Music (UK) and Chappell Warner Music (ROW).

"El Pueblo Vencera"
The People United Will Overcome

Join Amnesty International

Irish Section: 8 Shaw Street, Dublin 2

British Section: 5 Roberts Place, Bowling Green Lane, London EC1R OEJ

USA Section: P.O. Box 37137, Washington DC 20013

Australian Section: P.O. Box A159, Sydney South, N.S.W. 2000

> *"All the movies that I love are about intensity."*
>
> Phil Joanou.

Phil Joanou's film-making is fired by an unashamed passion seldom seen in the film industry. His boyish appearance and extraordinary enthusiasm have caused some amusement amid the supposed glamour of a Hollywood lifestyle, but this is one film director who just doesn't have time to worry about being cool. The film he is making is everything to him, and with the subject of his movie he clearly feels a kindred spirit.

"It's hard in music today to find a band that has intensity," Joanou says. "All the movies that I love are all about intensity —

The Godfather, Taxi Driver, Apocalypse Now — they all have this *driving* intensity, but there aren't many bands that have that. The Stones had it in the early days, The Who had it, The Clash had it for a while.

"The other thing is that when you look at, like, *Apocalypse Now,* which is maybe my favourite movie of all time, it not only has intensity it is also epic. To me that's what U2 are — intense and epic."

Joanou first met the band after a show in Hartford, Connecticut, and although they got on well, Joanou thought that was as far as it

Phil Joanou — Director

would go. "I never expected to make the U2 movie," he says, "I figured that if you're in U2's position you go with a big-name director. But I think the reason that we got along was that I wanted to find out what kind of movie they wanted to make. Instead of coming in and telling them how it should be done, I wanted to make the film *with* them.

"Sure enough, Bono did have in his head the kind of movie he wanted to do. Not the structure of the movie, but the feel, the tone, the mood. We talked for hours and in the end I said to them, 'If I were you, I'd get one of these three people to make your movie — Martin Scorsese, George Miller or Jonathan Demme — not me!'"

Shortly afterwards, the band asked Joanou to fly to Dublin to continue discussing the film. "That's when the real ideas started to become more concrete," he says. "The idea of there being both black & white and colour concert footage, and 16mm black & white documentary footage."

Joanou is an unorthodox director and fitted very well into U2's scheme of things. He not only directed the film but also edited it and operated one of the two documentary cameras himself. His "hands-on" approach reflects the way he first got into movie making. It was the most straightforward route of all — and he just did it.

"I started making Super 8 movies when I was 14," he says. "I didn't do the usual home-movie stuff. From the word go I was thinking of stories. I got all my friends to act in the stories and I made little scripts. They started off at three or four minutes, but by the time I was at senior high school I was making movies that were 45 minutes to an hour long.

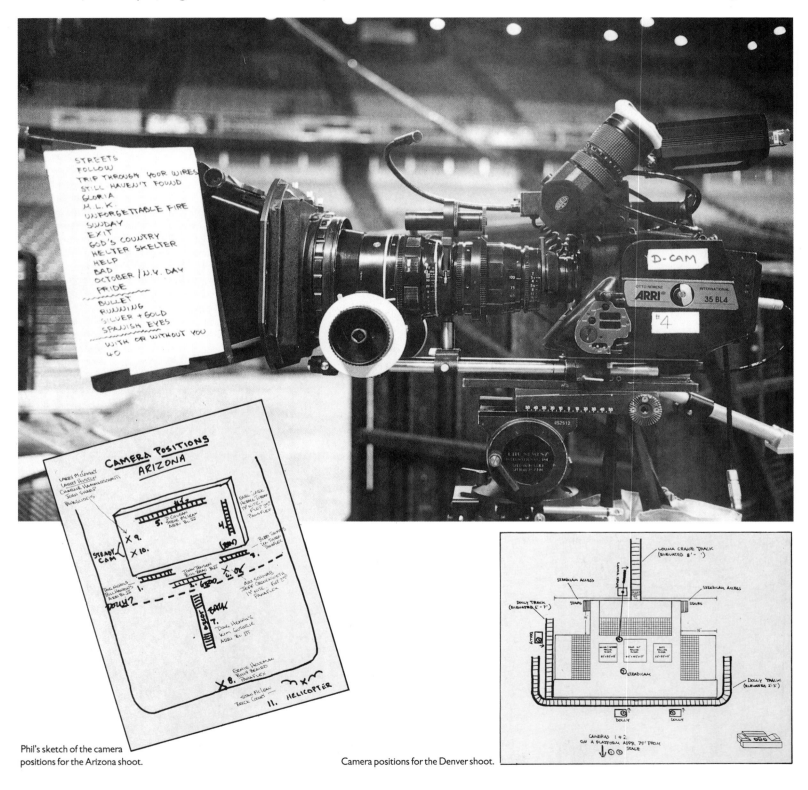

Phil's sketch of the camera positions for the Arizona shoot.

Camera positions for the Denver shoot.

"I was burning down my house, setting cars on fire, tossing dummies onto freeways... you name any psychotic act you could humanly perform with a camera and I did it in Super 8. I was hanging cameras off poles, out of car windows doing 80 miles per hour — I actually rode on the hood of a car going down a freeway to get a P.O.V. (point of view) shot.

"Later, I saved up and bought some editing equipment and continued to make films on my own until I went to theatre school at UCLA. While there I acted, directed and wrote plays rather than going straight into film-making, because I didn't want to become just a technician, I wanted to get a feel for emotion rather than just technique. Acting and working with actors in the theatre helped me develop that. That's still true now. With the U2 movie I want to get an emotional response out of the audience. I want to make them feel something, rather than just sit coolly in their seat and go 'oh, good soundtrack...'"

The label "Spielberg protégé" has been liberally applied to Joanou since the press picked up on the U2 movie. This description turns out to be somewhat inappropriate, and Joanou explains how he actually came to be involved with Spielberg.

"I went on to USC film school and started working with film up to 16mm. I made a 30 minute film for the end-of-year showing, and unbeknown to me, a representative of Steven Spielberg saw it and liked it. I had absolutely no cash at the time and had moved back to my parents house. The next day Steven Spielberg called me — on my parents phone. 'Hello, Phil Joanou? This is Steven Spielberg...' and I thought, this has *got* to be a joke!

"This was October 1984, and he asked me to direct two half-hour episodes of television, part of a series called *Amazing Stories*."

Once Joanou completed the two episodes, Spielberg asked him to come and work at his company, Amblin Entertainment, at the Universal Studios complex in Hollywood.

Joanou shot his first feature film, a comedy called *Three O'Clock High*, and before this even hit the cinemas, he was off with U2. The plan at Amblin had been that they would develop a script for Spielberg to produce and Joanou to direct, though what with U2 and other sidetracks this remains unrealised.

Always having been a fan of rock music, Joanou names three rock movies as his favourites:

"The best rock & roll documentary is definitely The Stones' *Gimme Shelter*, made by the Maysles Brothers in 1970. It grabs you in the first four minutes and keeps you there. No-one has done that before or since. The first film to be approached as one would a normal feature was Martin Scorsese's *The Last Waltz* with The Band. Then *Stop Making Sense* came along and blew everything else out of the water on a technical level. All three films are unique and they broke ground in the genre. That's one of our goals with *Rattle & Hum*. We'll see if we achieve it or not."

Joanou says that working with U2 has been a great experience for him, not only as a film director but also for him personally — to the point where he says it has "completely changed my direction as a film maker."

"When you work predominantly in the

Hollywood system you constantly get told that making money is the only way to measure success in film making. Once you make *Top Gun* a film maker is given an immense amount of power.

"When my first movie, *Three O'Clock High*, came out, and didn't break any box-office records I was really disappointed. I felt like I had failed. But the thing was, I was proud of the film, which was really confusing.

"I was really proud of what we were able to do — it was just a teen comedy, but I really felt good about the way we'd executed the movie and I felt we'd tried to do some things that hadn't been done in that genre before.

"The reviews were fine, no-one attacked me, everyone was pretty complimentary, but the movie didn't make money so I felt like it was all a mistake. The world I'd been in told me, 'make money, that's the way you win'. Money equals winning.

"But then I got out with U2 and spent time with them and saw their whole vibe on creating and so on — well, not in a pretentious way, but basically Money versus Art. Doing what comes out of your gut and not even thinking about the money. Doing it because you're passionate about it and letting the money follow or not follow. That's the way I'd always made films before I came to Hollywood and now I needed to get back to that: make quality films and the rest will follow. Being with U2 reminded me that I always have to make decisions based on what I'm passionate about — that's all that matters."

RATTLE & HUM

"I suppose it's a kind of photograph. It's not summing up U2, because no film or record could ever do that. We're not going to be staying where we are now. We're going to move on. We're going to change. Right now I hope · it captures what we're about, what we're doing musically and what happened to us on the road.

"It means a lot of people who couldn't get to the shows can still see us. If we went on the road for five years solid then maybe we could get to everyone who wants to see us, but we've no intention of doing that because it would have such a disastrous effect on our song writing not to mention our personal lives."

RATTLE & HUM

"In a way I think a band in transition is more interesting than a band at its destination. The going is more interesting than the getting there. One of the reasons the Joshua Tree Tour was so hard was the uncertainty about what U2 was. Yet that was one of the most interesting aspects of it."

RATTLE & HUM

*"I hope it gives people the feeling of
being close to the band. I hope that they'll see
that the band is a real thing and that they see
the friendship and the closeness of the band,
because that's the most important thing."*

RATTLE & HUM

"Concerning the movie, my only interest as a musician is that the music is right. I'm not sure a movie can capture your transition period. I think it's going to take a lot longer than that."

The *Joshua Tree* Tour

U2's *Joshua Tree* tour ran for 264 days, commencing and finishing in Tempe, Arizona in the USA. There were 110 shows at 72 venues in 15 countries, with a total ticketed attendance of 3,160, 998, plus an additional 20,000 or more at the San Francisco free concert.

DISCOGRAPHY

Albums:

BOY

Release Date:	October 1980
Catalogue Number:	ILPS 9646
Producer:	Steve Lillywhite
Track Listing:	I will follow / Twilight / Into the Heart / Out of Control / Stories for Boys / The Ocean / A Day Without Me / Another Time Another Place / The Electric Co. / Shadows and Tall Trees

OCTOBER

Release Date:	October 1981
Catalogue Number:	ILPS 9680
Producer:	Steve Lillywhite
Track Listing:	Gloria / I fall Down / I threw a brick through a window / Rejoice / Fire / Tomorrow / October / With a Shout / Stranger in a Strange Land / Scarlet / Is That All?

WAR

Release Date:	March 1983
Catalogue Number:	ILPS 9733
Producer:	Steve Lillywhite
Track Listing:	Sunday Bloody Sunday / Seconds / New Year's Day / Like a Song … / Drowning Man / The Refugee / Two Hearts Beat as One / Red Light / Surrender / "40"

THE UNFORGETTABLE FIRE

Release Date:	October 1984
Catalogue Number:	ILPS U25
Producer:	Brian Eno / Daniel Lanois
Track Listing:	A Sort of Homecoming / Pride / Wire / The Unforgettable Fire / Promenade / 4th of July / Bad / Indian Summer Sky / Elvis Presley and America / MLK

THE JOSHUA TREE

Release Date:	March 1987
Catalogue Number:	ILPS U26
Producer:	Daniel Lanois / Brian Eno
Track Listing:	Where the Streets have no Name / I Still Haven't Found What I'm Looking For / With or Without You / Bullet the Blue Sky / Running to Stand Still / Red Hill Mining Town / In God's Country / Trip Through Your Wires / One Tree Hill Exit / Mothers of the Disappeared

Singles

U2-3

Release Date:	September 1979
Catalogue Number:	CBS 7951
Producer:	Chas de Whalley / U2
Tracks:	Out of Control / Stories for Boys / Boy\Girl

ANOTHER DAY

Release Date:	September 1979
Catalogue Number:	CBS 8306
Producer:	Chas de Whalley
Tracks:	Another Day / Twilight

11 O' CLOCK TICK TOCK

Release Date:	May 1980
Catalogue Number:	WIP 6601
Producer:	Martin Hannett
Tracks:	11 O'Clock Tick Tock / Touch

A DAY WITHOUT ME

Release Date:	August 1980
Catalogue Number:	WIP 6601
Producer:	Steve Lillywhite
Tracks:	a Day Without Me / Things to make and do

I WILL FOLLOW

Release Date:	October 1980
Catalogue Number:	WIP 6656
Producer:	Steve Lillywhite
Tracks:	I Will Follow / Boy\Girl

FIRE

Release Date:	June 1981
Catalogue Number:	WIP 6679
Producer:	Steve Lillywhite
Tracks:	Fire/J. Swallow

(12" contained also 11 O'Clock Tick Tock/The Ocean-live. Double pack 7" contained also Cry/The Electric Co./11 O'Clock Tick Tock/The Ocean-live)

GLORIA

Release Date:	October 1981
Catalogue Number:	WIP 6733
Producer:	Steve Lillywhite
Tracks:	Gloria/I Will Follow (live)

A CELEBRATION

Release Date:	October 1982
Catalogue Number:	WIP 6770
Producer:	Steve Lillywhite
Tracks:	A Celebration/Trash, Trampoline and the Party Girl

NEW YEAR'S DAY

Release Date:	January 1983
Catalogue Number:	WIP 6848
Producer:	Steve Lillywhite
Tracks:	New Year's Day/Treasure

(Double pack contained also Fire/I Threw A Brick Through A Window/A Day Without Me-live)

TWO HEARTS BEAT AS ONE

Release Date:	March 1983
Catalogue Number:	IS 109
Producer:	Steve Lillywhite
Tracks:	Two Hearts Beat as One/Endless Deep

(12" & double pack 7" contained also New Year's Day/Two Hearts Beat as One - U.S. remixes)

PRIDE

Release Date:	September 1984
Catalogue Number:	IS 102
Producer:	Eno/Lanois
Tracks:	Pride/Boomerang

(12" contained also Boomerang II/4th of July)

THE UNFORGETTABLE FIRE

Release Date:	April 1985
Catalogue Number:	IS 220
Producer:	Eno/Lanois/Tony Visconti
Tracks:	The Unforgettable Fire/A Sort of Homecoming (live)

(12" also contained The Three Sunrises/Love Comes Tumbling. Double Pack 7" also contained Love Comes Tumbling/Sixty Seconds in Kingdom Come)

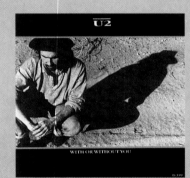

WITH OR WITHOUT YOU

Release Date:	March 1987
Catalogue Number:	IS 319
Producer:	Lanois/Eno
Mixed:	Steve Lillywhite
Tracks:	With or Without You/Luminous Times (Hold on to Love)/Walk to the Water

I STILL HAVEN'T FOUND WHAT I'M LOOKING FOR

Release Date:	May 1987
Catalogue Number:	IS 328
Producer:	Lanois/Eno
Tracks:	I Still Haven't Found What I'm Looking For/Spanish Eyes/Deep in the Heart

WHERE THE STREETS HAVE NO NAME

Release Date:	August 1987
Catalogue Number:	IS 340
Producer:	Lanois/Eno
Mixed:	Steve Lillywhite
Tracks:	Where The Streets Have No Name/Silver & Gold/Sweetest Thing/Race Against Time (12" & Cassette only)

IN GOD'S COUNTRY

Release Date:	November 1987 (USA only)
Catalogue Number:	7-99385
Producer:	Lanois/Eno
Tracks:	In God's Country/Bullet the Blue Sky/Running to Standstill

MINI L.P.'S

UNDER A BLOOD RED SKY

Release Date:	November 1983
Catalogue Number:	IMA 3
Producer:	Jimmy Iovine
Mixed:	Shelly Yakus
Tracks:	Gloria/11 O'Clock Tick Tock/I Will Follow/Party Girl/ Sunday Bloody Sunday/The Electric Co./New Year's Day/ "40"

WIDE AWAKE IN AMERICA

Release Date:	May 1985
Catalogue Number:	90279
Producer:	U2/Eno/Lanois/Tony Visconti
Tracks:	Bad (live)/A Sort of Homecoming (live)/The Three Sunrises/Love Comes Tumbling

VIDEOS

TITLE	DIRECTOR	LOCATION	DATE
Gloria	Meiert Avis	Dublin	October 1981
A Celebration	Meiert Avis	Kilmainham Jail, Dublin	April 1982
New Year's Day	Meiert Avis	Sweden	December 1982
Two Hearts Beat as One	Meiert Avis	Montmartre, Paris	March 1983
Under A Blood Red Sky	Gavin Taylor	Red Rocks, Denver, USA	June 1983
Pride (#1)	Donald Cammell	St Francis Xavier Hall, Dublin	August 1984
Pride (#2)	Barry Devlin	Slane Castle, Dublin	July 1984
Pride (#3)	Anton Corbijn	London	August 1984
A Sort of Homecoming	Barry Devlin	Paris, Brussells, Rotterdam, London, Glasgow	Oct/Nov 1984
Bad	Barry Devlin	Paris, Brussels, Rotterdam, London, Glasgow	Oct/Nov 1984
The Unforgettable Fire	Meiert Avis	Sweden	January 1985
With or Without You	Meiert Avis	Dublin	February 1987
Red Hill Mining Town	Neil Jordan	London	February 1987
Where The Streets Have No Name	Meiert Avis	Los Angeles	March 1987
In God's Country	Barry Devlin	Arizona	April 1987
I Still Haven't Found What I'm Looking For	Barry Devlin	Las Vegas	April 1987

PROPAGANDA is the official U2 magazine. It is only available by mail order.

One year's subscription costs:

To Ireland	IR£7.00 (Postal Orders Only)
To U.K.	Sterling £6.50
To U.S.A.	US$11.00
To Canada	US$14.00
To Europe	Sterling £8.00
Rest of World	
Surface Mail	Sterling £8.50
Air Mail	Sterling £11.00

Send a cheque or International Money Order payable to "PROPAGANDA" to:

The World (except North America):

U2 World Service
P.O. Box 18
Wellingborough
NN8 3YY
ENGLAND

USA/Canada:

U2 World Service
P.O. Box 806
New York
NY 10028
USA

During the live sequences of the movie the scale of the Arizona stadium show can be clearly seen. A U2 show has always been primarily about music, and about reaching the whole audience with that music. It's a simple idea, but on this scale it isn't such a simple task, so to give some idea of how this is achieved, here follows a listing of all of U2's on-stage equipment and the sound system used during a live show. All the same, it's worth remembering that at impromptu events like the San Francisco free concert, U2 can still get by without any of it!

ON-STAGE EQUIPMENT

Guitars:
Gibson Explorer
Gibson Les Paul (custom)
Fender Stratocaster (black)
Fender Stratocaster (sunburst)
Fender Telecaster
Danvel-Nelson Telecaster
Gibson 335
Squire Infinite Guitar
Fender Precision Bass
Ibanez Musician Bass
Fender Telecaster Bass
Gibson Thunderbird Bass
Zon Legacy Bass
Yamaha FG 365 II Acoustic
Yamaha L 20 A Acoustic
Gibson J160E Acoustic

Strings:
Superwound
Rotosound
James Howe Industries

Amps:
Vox AC30 (2)
Mesa Boogie
Roland JC120
BGW 750C Power Amp
BGW 250D Power Amp
Yamaha P2201 Power Amp
Yamaha P2050 Power Amp
Park Amplifier
Fender Deluxe Reverb (combo)

Speaker Cabinets:
Harbinger 516 (4)

Drums:
Yamaha Turbo Tour Custom Kit, comprising:
Yamaha Bass Drum BD824T
Yamaha 14" Piccolo Snare SD493
Yamaha Tom Tom TT814T
Yamaha Floor Tom FT916C (2)
Yamaha Floor Tom FT918C
plus:
Ludwig 13" Piccolo Snare
Latin Percussion Tito Puente Timbalis

Cymbals/Percussion:
Paiste 2002 14" Sound Edge Hi Hats
Paiste 3000 18" Rude Crash/Ride (2)
Paiste 2002 18" Heavy Crash
Paiste 2002 18" Medium
Latin Percussion Cow Bell
Latin Percussion Wood Block
Rhythm Tech Half Moon Tambourine (2)

Sticks:
Promark 5A ZX series

Keyboards:
Yamaha CP70 Midi Piano
Yamaha DX7-1 (2)
Yamaha DX7-2 FDR2
Yamaha RX5
Yamaha RX11
Roland SBX 10

Effects:
Yamaha SPX 90 (3)
Korg SDE 3000 (2)
Boss OD2 (2)
Memory Man Echo
Ibanez DM 1000
Ibanez VE 400
Brooks Infinite Sustain
Boss SCC 700
Boss SCC 700 C
ADA Digital Delay
Yamaha REV 7
KORG SDE 2000

Electronics:
Yamaha QX5 Sequencer (2)
Sycologic M16 Midi Patcher
TC Electronics TC 2290
AMS 1580S
Nady Transmitter/Receivers
Sony Transmitter/Receivers
Boss TU 12 Tuners
E Bow (2)

Pedals:
Moog Taurus Bass Pedals
Boss DD2
Boss FV 200
Boss DST
Korg DFS S/2
Vox Wah
Cry Baby Wah
Bass Turbo Overdrive
Ibanez C5 505
MXR Dyna Compressor
Poly Chorus
Boss DDS
Boss TOD 2
Boss FL 1

Furniture:
Yamaha Drum Stool

Reeds:
Horner Blues Harp

Vocals:
Shure SM58 Microphone
Vega Samson Radio Microphone
GML 300 Headset Microphone

THE JOSHUA TREE TOUR
P.A. SPECIFICATIONS

Clair Bros. Audio S4 system with sub-low bass system

INDOOR ARENA SYSTEM:

72 S4 cabinets
12 Sub-low cabinets
Full 360 degree flying system

OUTDOOR STADIUM SYSTEM:

144 S4 cabinets
24 Sub-low cabinets
12 R4 front fills

P.A. CONTROL SYSTEM:

2 Clair Bros. Consoles
Clair Bros. Crossover system
Clark-Technic Graphics
System Protection — DBX 160
Speaker System — JBL
Amplifier Power — Carver

F.O.H. EFFECTS-TREATMENTS

1	LEXICON 224XL Digital Reverb
1	LEXICON 200 Digital Reverb
1	LEXICON 97 Super Prime Time D.D.L.
3	LEXICON PCM 70 Multi Effects Processor
1	A.M.S. DMX 1580S Digital Delay Harmonizer
2	Roland SDE 3000 D.D.L.
1	RAINE 6-way splitter (sub-low feed Distribution)

Housed in 3 x DBX 900 series racks:

14	DBX 904 Noise Gates
3	DBX 903 Comp/Limiters
4	DBX 902 DE/Essers
4	DBX 905 Par/EQ
3	DBX 165 Comp/Limiters
2	DBX 160 2 Channel Comp/Limiters

CLAIR CONSOLE "A"

Channel	Instrument	Mic
1	Kick Drum	M88
2	Snare Top	M88
3	Snare Bottom	SM57
4	Hi-hat	SM81
5	Rack Tom Tom	M88
6	Timbale	Sen421
7	Picalo Snare (S.R.)	SM57
8	Floor Tom Tom	M88
9	Mounted Rack Tom Tom	M88
10	Picalo Snare (S.L.)	SM57
11	Tamborines	SM56
12	Percussion	SM57
13	Overhead Cymbals (S.R.)	SM81
14	Overhead Cymbals (S.L.)	SM81
15	Sim Kick Left	F.O.H.
16	Sim Kick Right	F.O.H.
17	Sim Snare Left	F.O.H.
18	Sim Snare Right	F.O.H.
19	Sim Rack Tom	F.O.H.
20	Sim Floor Tom	F.O.H.
21	Sim Floor 3 (Mounted Rack Tom)	F.O.H.
22	Precision Bass 1	D.I.
23	Precision Bass 2	D.I.
24	Telecaster Bass 3	D.I.
25	Bass Pedals	D.I.
26	Bass Effects	D.I.
27	Harbinger Spkr Hi	RE20
28	Harbinger Spkr Lo	RE20
29	RX11 - Kick Drum	D.I.
30	RX11 - Snare Drum	D.I.
31	RX11 - Tom Tom Drum	D.I.
32	RX11 - Stereo Mix	D.I.

CONSOLE "A" BUSS SENDS:

Send	Effect/Treatment	Returns
1	Lexicon 200 Digital Reverb	1 + 2
2	PCM 70-A Digital Processor	3 + 4
3	PCM 70-B Digital Processor	5 + 6
4	Sub Low Feed	Buss Outputs

CONSOLE "A" F.O.H. INSERT PATCHING:

Channel	Instrument	Effect
1	Kick Drum	DBX 904 + DBX 903
2	Snare Top	DBX 904
3	Snare Bottom	DBX 904
4	Hi-Hat	DBX 904
5	Rack Tom Tom	DBX 904
6	Timbale	DBX 904
7	Picalo Snare S.R.	DBX 904
8	Floor Tom Tom	DBX 904
9	Mounted Rack Tom Tom	DBX 904
10	Picalo Snare S.L.	DBX 904
11	Tambourines	DBX 904
12	Percussion	DBX 904
22	Precision Bass 1	DBX 165
23	Precision Bass 2	DBX 165
24	Telecaster Bass 3	DBX 165
25	Bass Pedals	DBX 160
26	Bass Effects	DBX 160

CONSOLE "A" SUB GROUPS:

1 Kick - Snare
2 Tom Toms
3 Simmons
4 Drum Treatments
5 RX - 11
6 Bass Guitar

CLAIR CONSOLE "B"

Channel	Instrument	Mic.
1	T.F. Rack Left Key Mix	D.I.
2	T.F. Rack Right Key Mix	D.I.
3	Sony F1 Left Pre-Show Music P.B.	F.O.H.
4	Sony F1 Right Pre-Show Music P.B.	F.O.H.
5	Sony C.D. Left Pre-Show Music P.B.	F.O.H.
6	Sony C.D. Left Pre-Show Music P.B.	F.O.H.
7	Cassette Pre-Show Music P.B.	F.O.H.
8	Shimmer Guitar Treatment	D.I.
9	E-MAX Left Keyboard	D.I.
10	E-MAX Right Keyboard	D.I.
11	DX7 - 1 Keyboard	D.I.
12	DX7 - 2 Keyboard	D.I.
13	CP70 Piano Dry	D.I.
14	CP70 Piano Treatment	D.I.
15	Keyboard Amp	SM57
16	Edge Acoustic Guitar	D.I.
17	Guitar 1 VOX AC30 - 1	SM57
18	Guitar 2 Mesa Boogie	SM57
19	Guitar 3 VOX AC30 - 2	SM57
20	Bono Acoustic Guitar	D.I.
21	Bono Guitar Amp	SM57
22	Larry Tom Tom (Front of Stage)	Sen 421
23	Larry Vocal - headset mic	GML 300
24	Adam Vocal	SM58
25	Edge Vocal	SM58
26	Piano Vocal	SM58
27	Bono Spare Vocal	SM58
28	Bono Wireless / Radio Vocal	Vega - Samson
29	Bono Main Vocal	SM58
30	S.D.E. 3000 Digital Delay Effect	F.O.H.
31	PCM 70 Left Digital Reverb	F.O.H.
32	PCM 70 Right Digital Reverb	F.O.H.

CLAIR CONSOLE "B" BUSS SENDS:

Send	Effect / Treatment	Returns
1	AMS DMX 1580SW D.D.L.	1 + 2
2	LEXICON 97 Super Prime Time D.D.L.	3 + 4
3	LEXICON 224 XL Digital Reverb	5 + 6
4	PCM 70 Digital Multi FXs Processor	31 + 32

CONSOLE "B" F.O.H. INSERT PATCHING:

Channel	Instrument	Effect
9	E-MAX Left Keyboard	Sub-Low Feed
10	E-MAX Right Keyboard	Sub-Low Feed
11	DX7 - 1 Keyboard	Sub-Low Feed
12	DX7 - 2 Keyboard	Sub-Low Feed
22	Larry Tom Tom Front of Stage	DBX 904
25	Edge Vocal	DBX 902
	Insert SDE 3000	DBX 903
		DBX 905
27	Bono Sapre Vocal	DBX 160
		DBX 902
		DBX 905
28	Bono Wireless - Radio Vocal	DBX 160
		DBX 902
		DBX 905
29	Bono Main Vocal	
	Insert SDE 3000	DBX 902
		DBX 903
		DBX 905

CONSOLE "B" SUB GROUPS:

1 Vocals
2 Drums
3 Bass
4 Guitar
5 Keyboards
6 Effects

U2: Rattle & Hum was filmed between September 1987 and July 1988. The producer was Michael Hamlyn for Midnight Films, the director was Phil Joanou, executive producer was Paul McGuinness. The film was produced by Midnight Films, Los Angeles and London. Gregg Fienberg was associate producer and production manager, production being co-ordinated by Fiona Dent. London production executives were Iain Brown and Juliet Naylor. Assisting Phil Joanou was Carol Johnson. The directors of photography were Jordan Cronenweth A.S.C. for the colour photography and Robert Brinkmann for the black & white. The colour concert footage was filmed at the Sun Devils Stadium in Tempe, Arizona, on December 19th & 20th 1987. It was filmed on 35mm Kodak 5294 high speed colour negative film, rated at 400ASA, using four Panaflex Gold cameras, three Arri BL IV's, one Arri BL III, one Panaglide, one Steadicam plus another Panaglide mounted in a helicopter. These were operated by Bobby Thomas, Doug Nichol, Earl Clark, Art Schwab, John Jensen, Dick Coleman, Ernie Holzman, David Henning on the Louma Crane, Larry McConky on the Steadicam, Charlie Hammerschmitt on the Panaglide and Stan McClain up in the helicopter. Gaffer was Colin Campbell, key grip was Cary Griffith, and the camera assistants were Jeff Cronenweth, William Hankins, Jon Sharp, Billy Broa, Billy Baird, Horace Jordan, Don Thorn Jnr., Kim Guthrie, Larry Houston, Steve McClain and Brek Cooney. On the second night a twelfth camera was added operated by Robert Brinkmann and assisted by Richard Osbourne. The 2nd camera assistants in Arizona were Michael Selph and Alan Cohen. The film loaders were Jimmy Jensen, Mick McClain, Kate Hall, Colin Crane & Christa Wallace. Production co-ordinator was Suzanne Marlow and the assistant directors were Chuck Connor and Michael Helfand. The head film runner was Cole Campbell and the stills were taken by Bill Rubenstein. The black & white concert footage was filmed in McNichols Arena, Denver, Colorado on the 7th & 8th of November 1987, using 35mm Kodak 5222 Double X high speed black & white negative film. There were a total of eight cameras, all of which were Arri BL IV's, except for the Steadicam which was an Arri III. The camera operators were Doug Nichol, Marc Reshovsky, Michael McClary Sandy Chandler, Jeff Zimmerman, David Henning on the Louma Crane and Larry McConky on the Steadicam.

The eighth camera was locked on wide angle, and had an assistant to monitor it, but no operator. It was used on the second night of Denver only. Gaffer was Martin Coppen and key grip was Greg Hoffman. The camera assistants were William Hankins, Dave Rudd, Joe Antczak, Umberto De Luna, Derek Scott, Bill Coss on the Louma, Larry Houston on the Steadicam and Michael Price on camera 8. The film loaders at Denver were Laurie White, Jeremy Briggs, Chris Faloona and Robert Smith. Here too, Bill Rubenstein was the stills photographer. Peter Williams designed the original stage lighting and operated the lighting system on the night. Most of the documentary footage was filmed on two cameras, with a third and fourth one being added occasionally for sequences like the San Francisco free gig. The documentary cameras were Arri 16 SR's, operated by Phil Joanou and Robert Brinkmann, assisted by Joe Antczak and Laurie White, Jeremy Briggs was the loader. The rest of the documentary crew were Kaaren Ochoa — production, Michael Dellheim — location advance, Steve Molen, Al Hersh and Gary Hardman — transportation. Otto Nemenz International custom built the zoom controls into the 16mm camera handles to make them easier to use on the run. The film stock was 16mm Kodak 7231 Plus X medium speed black & white negative film and 16mm Kodak 7222 Double X high speed negative film. Kodak had to make an extra batch of 16mm Double X to supply enough for the movie. The amount of film used for the concert shoots was 210,000 feet of 35mm colour film and 125,000 feet of 35mm black & white film. The documentary used a total of 250,000 feet of 16mm film, which when transferred to 35mm is the equivalent of 625,000 feet, giving an overall total of 960,000 feet. If shown continuously at 24 frames per second, this would last for 1 week, 9 hours, 46 minutes and 40 seconds — enough to make one hundred and eighteen 90-minute movies. Duart Laboratory in New York processed the black & white, Deluxe in Hollywood processed the colour and Technicolor in Universal City made the prints. Documentary sound was recorded by William MacPherson C.A.S. and George Baetz. The concert film editing was done by transferring the footage to time-coded video tape and using six ¾" off-line VTR's, computer-synchronised in real time, making it possible to view six camera angles at once. The editor was Phil Joanou, film editing staff were Tom Seid, Ken Blackwell and Lori Eshler. It took 10 months to sync the film with the sound, with Liz Shore being the key assistant editor. The sound effects were created by Blue Light Sound, supervising sound editor was Scott Hecker, music editors were Bob Badami and Bill Bernstein. In Denver and Arizona, house audio engineer was, as always, Joe O'Herlihy, who co-ordinated all the live recording. The concert soundtracks were recorded on the Manor Mobile, the Pumacest Advision Mobile and Remote Recording Services Inc. mobile recording studios, using overlapping 24 track machines, with 48 track capability. Recording was engineered by Tom Ponunizio, unit engineers at various times were Dave Hewitt and Mark Wallis. Steve Lillywhite did some of the recording in Europe. Brian Reeves was the movie sub mix down engineer. Chris Jenkins was the mixer for the final mix.

For the *Desire* session at the Point Depot in Dublin the engineer was Dave Meegan assisted by Pat MacCarthy, the unit engineer was Gary Stewart. For the *Little Angel of Harlem* session at Sun Studio, the engineers were Cowboy Jack Clements and David Ferguson. The entire soundtrack was produced by Jimmy Iovine and mixed at A & M studios in Los Angeles. U2's tour manager was Dennis Sheehan, production manager was Steve Iredale, assisted by Tom Mullally, stage managers were Tim Buckley and Jake Kennedy. Des Broadbery looked after the keyboards, Dallas Schoo looked after The Edge's guitars, Fraser McAlister looked after all the bass gear, Sam O'Sullivan looked after drum world and Bob Loney looked after all things electronic. The outdoor staging was engineered by John McHugh. For the Arizona film shoot the stage was completely rebuilt to accommodate all the extra equipment and ended up being 200' wide and 80' deep. It was erected by Spike Falana, Dave Lewis, Shane McCarthy, Darren Stoner, Warren Jones, Gem Dumble, Neil Hickey, Pat Ledwith, Steve Coton, Chris Roberts, Michael Kerr and Keith Hughes. The design for the scrims and drapes was first drawn by The Edge in a dressing room in Pontiac, MI, and later finished by Jeremy Thom. These were then made by Kimpton Walker in London. The indoor staging was conceived by Steve Iredale, Peter Williams and Tim Buckley, re-vamped by U2, engineered by Jeremy Thom, fabricated by Tait Towers Inc. and constructed daily by Dragan Kuzmanov and A. J. Rankin who also paged Bono's mic cable.

The stage was 5' high, 74' wide and 48' deep. The drum riser was 10' x 12' x 2', the keyboard and bass risers were both 8' x 8' x 6", Wardrobe was by Lola Cashman and the haircuts were done by Fintan Fitzgerald. Security was in the hands of Bob Wein, John Clark, Mike Andy and Jim Singleton. Much of the co-ordination went through Principle Management in New York, handled by Ellen Darst and Keryn Kaplan. Press was handled by Paul Wasserman and Regine Moylett, Suzanne Doyle dealt with the unbelievable number of guests. O. J. Kilkenny & Co. take care of U2's accounts. On tour accounts were handled by Bob Koch and Rich Glasgow. The Dublin co-ordination was handled by Ned O'Hanlon, Anne Louise Kelly and Barbara Galavan. Lighting crew for Nocturne Inc. were Ed Hyatt, Scott Richmond, Geoff Dickey, Jon Jewett, Barry Claxton, Robert Margoshes, Fred Watson, Gabe Fielding, Jeff Stange, Kevin McMullen, Robert Cooper and John Lobel. Sound crew for Clair Brothers were Jo Ravitch, C. J. Patterson, Billy Louthe, Tom Giannoni, Gino, Jeff Stein, Sean McGovern and Boomer, with onstage sound by Keith Carroll and Dave Skaff. Riggers were Steve Witmer, Bill Spoon and Gary Currier, Mike Esmonde did the advance production. The huge number of trucks were driven by John Herbert, Cody Chase, Larry Duff, Bruce Burrows, Mike Wazorick, Rich Krouldis, Randy Johnson, Dale Macon, Wayne Singer, Mike Reed, Peter Semeniuk, Ken Devore, Lee Malone, Curt Williams, Zeke Zilkowski, Mickey Lloyd, Robert Vaughan, Marion Shelton, Robert Frost, Bill James, Scott Lawson, Doug Williams, Bob Plankis, Steve Gasper, David Greene, Gary Rogers, Chris Anderson, Bob Sullivan, John Iniguez, Leonard Lopez, Marc Coen, Dan Hogan, Ray Underwood, Monty Lindbergh, Paul Dana, Ron Saulter, Judy Saulter, Albert Carusillo, Michael De Contreras and A. J. Cavallari. The buses were driven by Jack Lapp, Rufus Crockett, Red Julian and Renaine Julian. Travel was looked after by Trinifold Travel and Leeds Travel. Air travel by Nigel White. Arthur Devries and Kurt Walters flew the band's plane, Robin Pittock, Roger Woolsey and Jeannie Pittock flew the management Viscount.

This book was edited and compiled by Peter Williams and designed by Steve Averill for Works Associates — Dublin. Steve Turner was the guest writer. Chris Parkes co-ordinated the book for U2, Piers Murray Hill co-ordinated for Octopus Publishers but the whole book would not have come together were it not for Anne Louise Kelly. Most of the photographs were taken by Colm Henry and Bill Rubenstein, but the others are listed elsewhere. U2 wrote most of the songs in the film, except for one by The Beatles, one by Bob Dylan and a little of one by Elvis. Bono sang most of the songs and played harmonica and guitar. The Edge also sang as well as playing guitars and keyboards. Adam Clayton played bass guitar and pedals. Drums, percussion and backing vocals were by Larry Mullen Jnr.